The Affirmation Web
A Believe in Yourself Adventure

By Lori Lite
Illustrated by
Helder Botelho

Specialty Press, Inc.
Florida

Library of Congress Cataloging-in-Publication Data

Lite, Lori, 1961-

The affirmation web: a believe in yourself adventure / by Lori Lite :
Illustrated by Helder Botelho
        p.   cm.
Summary: A sad, lonely young girl follows a group of animals in
the forest as they weave a web of positive thoughts and statements
about themselves, making her feel special as well.

        ISBN 1-886941-25-4
        [1. Self-esteem—Fiction.   2. Animals — Fiction.]
        I. Botelho, Helder, ill.   II. Title
        PZ7.L6975Af   1997   97-26752
        [Fic] — dc21

Published by Specialty Press, Inc.
300 N.W. 70th Avenue, Suite 102
Plantation, Florida 33317
(954) 792-8100

Manufactured in China.
Production Location: Guangdong, China
Production Date: 11/11/09
Cohort: Batch 1

I dedicate this book to Tarin, Austin,

Jemma and children everywhere,

that they may shine and sparkle

and be all that they were born to be.

Congratulations!

You have taken a wonderful step in bringing affirmations to your child. As a child I believed that the moon followed me home. I was that self-assured, that confident. I liked myself that much. Now your child can have that same feeling. With repeated use of this book you will see your child's self-esteem grow. You'll see your child believe in him/herself, and you'll see your child live a healthier life.

Once your child is comfortable with affirmations try choosing affirmations for specific situations. For instance, if your child is having nightmares try these affirmations: "I am safe," and "I will sleep peacefully." Always use positive words in affirmations. Try affirmations on the way to school. For example try "I will learn easily" and "I will follow directions."

With daily use, affirmations can transform your child's life. For an added benefit try using the "Affirmation Web" after reading "A Boy and a Bear." These two books work beautifully together as your child will learn breathing for relaxation while being able to recite affirmations.

Every child deserves a life filled with self-confidence and wellness. I thank God for the opportunity to believe that the moon follows me home. I hope that my books fill your child with that same magic.

Look for my next book in this relaxation series, "A Boy and a Turtle." This book will introduce your child to visualization techniques and will complete the relaxation series.

Lori Lite

A girl sat in the woods feeling sad and lonely.

A bird who had been watching the girl decided to share a secret with her.

The bird swooped down from the trees
and whispered in her ear, "Follow me and
you will see just how special life can be."

The girl, filled with curiosity, quickly followed the bird.

She leaped over branches,

splashed through streams,

climbed over rocks,

and dodged around trees.

Until finally the bird came to rest . . .
right next to a spider busy at work.

The spider lowered himself to the girl's shoulder and whispered in her ear, "My friends and I are strong and proud. Just say nice things to yourself out loud."

An opossum spiraled down from a branch above. She placed herself across from the girl and said, "I am beautiful."

And with that the spider danced over to the opossum leaving behind a sparkling trail of web.

A mole emerged from his deep dark hole. He placed himself across from the opossum and said, "I am healthy."

And with that the spider danced
over to the mole leaving behind
a sparkling trail of web.

A snake slithered out from under the
leaves. He placed himself across from the
mole and said, "I am gentle and kind."

And with that the spider danced
over to the snake leaving behind
a sparkling trail of web.

A butterfly fluttered down on a breeze. She placed herself across from the snake and said, "I can be still."

And with that the spider danced over to the butterfly leaving behind a sparkling trail of web.

A porcupine wandered over to the group. She placed herself across from the butterfly and said, "I am smart."

And with that the spider danced over
to the porcupine leaving behind a
sparkling trail of web.

A bat circled above their heads. He placed himself across from the porcupine and said, "I am forgiving of myself and others."

And with that the spider danced over
to the bat leaving behind a sparkling
trail of web.

A skunk stepped shyly to the circle of friends. She placed herself across from the bat and said, "I like myself."

And with that the spider danced
over to the skunk leaving behind
a sparkling trail of web.

A squirrel completed the circle of friends. He placed himself among them all and said, "I believe in myself."

And with that the spider danced over
to the squirrel completing the web.

With strength and confidence the circle of friends lifted their sparkling web to the sun.

The girl stepped forward.
She whispered for all their ears to hear,

"Thank you for sharing affirmations
this way."

*"My life is more special
beginning today!"*

Here are some more affirmations for you to experience.
Choose what feels good to you.

- I am happy.
- I am creative.
- I am strong.
- I am peaceful.
- I am polite.
- I am unique.
- I am talented.
- I am special.
- I am loved.
- I follow directions.
- I am confident in myself.
- I learn easily.
- I pay attention.
- I am calm.
- I am safe.
- I am relaxed.
- I sleep peacefully.

Now that you've experienced **The Affirmation Web**, you can help the web grow by reading this story to more children. Many times parents are invited to read to their child's class. This is a perfect opportunity to teach children about affirmations.

After you read the book, have the children sit in a circle like the characters in the book. Take out a ball of yarn. Say an affirmation, hold the end of the yarn and pass the ball of yarn across the circle. That child will now say an affirmation and hold on to a piece of the yarn while passing the ball across the circle to another child. As each child holds on to the yarn a web begins to grow. They create their own affirmation web. The children also love to lift their sparkling web to the sun. I've been told that even teenagers enjoy this activity.

I had the opportunity to weave a web at my son's class for Halloween. I used orange and black yarn and the children never even missed the candy. Instead they went home with a bag full of self esteem.

Try weaving Christmas webs, Chanukah webs, and Valentine webs, and give the gift of affirmations!

Lori Lite